FIRST EDITION

www.ttclife.org/tiffygabs

#CRUSHTHEDAY

#TIFFYGABS

The art of surviving any trauma is in knowing that you are still relevant to the areas you are built to impact if you have the courage to heal.

This is how I made it.
#crushtheday

xoxo
Tiffy Gabs

If the clock stops ...it might not be as simple as replacing the battery ...

So I heard you felt a little stuck, a little paused, in a rut, with your capacity frozen in the place where you've lost your drive to keep going. It might have been a slow systematic stream of events... or maybe it's just one crushing reality that you can't find a way to get over.

Somewhere in your mind, you know when you lost your momentum because your hands have marked the time. The time when you lost the most precious thing in your life, the time when you failed miserably, the time when you lost yourself trying to be everything but you. .... BUT YOU my dear are still in there. Today is the day where we tackle this thing together. Page by page, prayer by prayer, here is our opportunity to face this thing safely in the exchange of your thoughts and mine. Make this your own, I've made room for you, your thoughts, your secrets, your prayers and the new things you will start saying to yourself.

Some things are not as simple as they seem and may require more than the quick fixes offered to you to lighten the mood. They require honesty, an ear that is not intimidated by the truth and a heart that is willing to do the work. Today you will not feel the pressure to be better for everyone but to truly take the time to do the work and heal. So before you turn the next page let's make a pact and establish our foundation together.

Identify it

Face the thing that is affecting you. Don't suppress it or deny that it is there, Give your soul permission to open up, call it out and give it a name. Whether it was a series of events or just one face it

Come unto me, all ye that labour and are heavy laden, and I will give you rest.
Matthew 11:28 KJV

Process the Pain

Pain doesn't make you weak it just reminds you that you are still alive. You are paused because you are afraid that moving forward will hurt. So cry about the past, God is not afraid of your tears but know that your future does not have to paralyze you because your arms worked fine before the trauma. Scream if you have to, take it out in the gym, take long walks in places your tears can fall but above all give it to God. Prayer is a place to empty your soul of its wounds and heal it with the words of your Creator.

.Casting all your care upon him; for he careth for you." **1 Peter 5:7 KJV**

Forgive Yourself

Sometimes the greatest hurdle is overcoming the responsibility of your part in the pain. The people you've let in, the ones you let slip away, the wisdom you ignored, the choice you made.

I see you thinking about it... not that easy to let it go now is it? I know I played the death of my daughter over and over again in my head every day. I could not see my capacity to do good or make good decisions or be someone anyone could love but I had to forgive myself. I had to be OK with the fact that I can mature beyond my deficits and become treasure but it all started with me saying sorry to the girl in the mirror and believing that she would change.

"And he said unto me, My grace is sufficient for thee: for my strength is made perfect in weakness ..."
2 Corinthians 12:9a KJV

Breathing is the evidence that God has not given up on you and even when you feel like you can't God promises to breathe new life in you by His Spirit. God's grace is greater than anything.

Forgive Others

There will come a point where we have to let go the bitterness associated with the people that have hurt us. There are so many factors that contribute to any decisive or impulsive action: the past, the environment, needs, wants, core values and perceptions. God is the only entity that is aware of all the factors at play. We are neither omniscient nor omnipresent so we are limited to what we know. Believe that just like you, each person is in a different stage of development and be willing to release the former idea of an individual to embrace their growth. Bitterness keeps us stuck and rusted at the place of error limiting ourselves to the emotions of the past. Do you like feeling angry about this all the time or do you want that 10,000lb feeling to go? It doesn't take perfect conditions to move on, it just takes a decision. God wants us to value our freedom as much as He does.

Don't feed the dysfunction any longer. You know that some of the people you are still angry about have moved, died or forgotten completely about the situation. It's time for you to embrace the fact that closure may come on your own. Maybe you need to write down the things you wanted to say and never got to. Get it out of your system. Then discard that page in a permanent way. ...Just burn it... without burning down the house OK... good.

Make a promise to yourself to stop rehearsing the situation and file it in lessons learned. That person did not make a great choice at that time but pray that they've grown beyond it and if they have not they still have time to learn. You are not responsible for the pace of someone else's development, just let it go.

For if ye forgive men their trespasses, your heavenly Father will also forgive you: But if ye forgive not men their trespasses, neither will your Father forgive your trespasses.
St Matthew 16:14-15 KJV

Find Your Battery

This will be your final stage in the process. It is only when you're healed that you can make use of things that are meant to build you in a sustainable way. Finding the real source of what makes you function gives you the power to restart but without complete healing the power may cause further damage. Think of that person on your job that is responsible for the care of a team and are given the tools and the muscle to run it. Exciting isn't it... until you discover that they have trust issues.

You may not know this yet but the persons around you that you love and care for are feeling the effects of your hurt through the walls you build up, those defensive weapons of mass destructions and the land mines surrounding anything that reminds you of your pain.

Clock the time and learn from it. Clock the time and grieve through it but don't rust. Don't ever feel like you should be discarded because you stopped, there is still more in you. The trauma can affect you, it may even infect your perspective but it can never change who you really are and what you can do.

God's word is active and living. It speaks beyond our failures and bring us right back to the manufacturer's design. Let's go back to the manual, restore what's missing or out of place and then you'll be ready for power. How many volts from God do you require? He knows but He molds before He empowers. God is not afraid of your brokenness because He is the only one qualified to restore.

But if the Spirit of him that raised up Jesus from the dead dwell in you, he that raised up Christ from the dead shall also quicken your mortal bodies by his Spirit that dwelleth in you.

Romans 8:11 KJV

Let's do the Work!

Identify it!

Prayer Time

Lord heal my broken places. I pour out every place of hurt bitterness, disappointment, rejection, grief, emptiness, guilt and shame before You. Help me to forgive those that have hurt me and help me to forgive myself. Open my heart to receive new life in Jesus name.
AMEN

Declaration

My pain will not define me. My purpose is still in my pieces. God will help me put them back together

Notes

Sometimes moving forward

starts with identifying what's missing

What did you really lose along the way beyond the obvious things that you've told everybody? It's not just the loved one, not just the marriage, not just the friendship, the house or the job. Those things are gone but the things you lost are hanging around somewhere; you just can't locate them. Let's look a little closer at the springs and cogs on the inside; the trust, confidence, faith, hope... that positive outlook you had on life that everything was going to work has suddenly vanished because of this one moment.

Face the reality that obvious things you lost may never come back to you but those inner bolts and screws... they sure can with improvements. You may never be able to revive that relationship that has you eating pints of ice-cream and snarling at everyone that dares to look in your direction but your capacity to love although bruised, is not broken. It just needs to be re-established with some boundaries.

And said, Naked came I out of my mother's womb, and naked shall I return thither: the Lord gave, and the Lord hath taken away; blessed be the name of the Lord.**Job 1:21 KJV**

We look at this scripture and somehow we believe that it is about everything that we have built along the way. That just like our car we bought on credit our emotions were on loan to us from a bank called trust. Naked is not synonymous with nothing. Naked means unclothed, unmasked, no barriers, no defense mechanism just raw and open. No matter how guarded you have become in life; it is God's intent for us to return to that nakedness that doesn't make us ashamed of who we are. Who told you that you were cold? Who told you that you were exposed? Who told you that you were not enough? Take the time to tell God about the snakes in your garden messing with your mind. God wants to you to move in a garden of snakes and not lose your dominion to shame because who you are is settled in Him.

When you came into this world you were given a full capacity to trust, hope, love, have faith, be secure, establish a sense of worth and confidence. However by reason of use and through a series of interactions these screws become loose if they are not serviced. What are you doing right now to maintain your peace, joy, the things that hold you together?

If we are really honest although some of these grounding pieces are still there they have become dysfunctional because of indents left behind by trauma, mistakes and disappointments. Some things are laying at the site of impact and we have to revisit that place and gain closure. There is a place in your life that needs to function again. Your joy, your peace, your confidence, your ability to take another negative thing in your life can be put back in place when we understand what healing really means.

Healing challenges us to not only identify our brokenness but claim back the mechanisms that make us work. God can and will restore. Imagine this God was willing to squeeze His infinite being into a finite body to restore the mechanism that allows us to connect with Him. The greatest trauma experienced by man was sin and if you trace any trauma you experience right now a little sin is in the blow. Sin attempts to rob you of innocence, strips your ability to connect to those that mean you well, isolates you from former places of dominion and brings shame.

Listen we are going to be real on these pieces of paper today. Whether you are the victim or the perpetrator: healing is available for you because although no one says it on the inside it is a FACT that while we are wounding others; we are wounding ourselves.

Let's take that step that makes us feel vulnerable, you know naked and open. You won't start ticking again until you retrieve the things laying at the scene of the crime. Until you have the bravery to revisit that place, admit to yourself that you let your faith go right there, that your belief went down in the casket with your loved one, that you signed away your peace on that divorce paper and people have moved on with your pieces in their luggage, driven off with them in their car and carried them to the grave you will remain stuck. My dear look yourself in the mirror and make a decision to ask God for the courage to go get yourself back.

It is possible to lose the very essence of who you are because of pain. I remember the many days I became the dead baby's Mom; walking through the supermarket and people pointing at me "Oh there she is, the lady on the TV."

It was like I had lost my name my spark, shrouded in black with a well appointed pair of pumps. I know what it's like to struggle to do the things regular Moms do so easily because it reminded me that my daughter was not there and having to push through so that my remaining child who was still alive could have a Mom that was present enough to love her too. God had to remind me that I was still in there and that the tears I shed would never be enough to drown who I really was inside...Tiffany Gabrielle

Hope deferred maketh the heart sick: but when the desire cometh, it is a tree of life
Proverbs 13:12.

God can bring back your desire to live, to move, and to operate in the truth of who you are. You my friend can stand naked and not ashamed having others experience the full definition of who you are without barriers or filters.

God is the only entity that can help you recover what you have truly lost because He is the one that has intricately designed you and put you together. No one else truly knows what you are truly missing. The problem with pain is that help can only be effective when the pain can be defined clearly and accurately. Understanding the pain is limited to your ability to define it but God's understanding is limitless. He is intricately connected with you and what you are going through . He was there when it happened and He knows every side of your story.

As you connect with these pages, find a place to pray. Prayer empties the soul of indescribable ills. Prayer connects us to an omnipotent source that has enough grace to help no matter how bad the situation is. Prayer can hold our deepest darkest secrets and grasp our ugliest truths and present them to a God that is not ashamed of us but forgives us back to life.

I wish you knew that the times you heard your mother crying it was not always to ask God to put food on the table or help you afford a new shirt. I wish you knew the groans of your father was not always about the money or the house. The greatest need of man is a place where no human can touch, where no drug can anesthetize. You can come to terms with it with a therapist but only God can restore it... who you really are on the inside

Nobody may know what you are doing to be functional right now. Maybe you have resorted to isolation, drinking, work, drugs, a pursuit of excellence but that emptiness you're feeling is an indication that something is still missing. Stop fighting the truth. Life happens to everyone but no one understands it better than the author of life itself... God

Let's do the Work!

What's Missing?

Prayer Time

Lord I submit myself to you, the things that are open and that which is hidden. I lay my burden upon you. You are strong enough to hold my tears, caring enough to grant me Your shoulder to lean on, patient enough to wait on this moment. I open my heart to you. Locate my missing pieces and restore my soul, AMEN

Declaration

Everything I was in the beginning is still within me. My purpose is not dead. God has not changed His mind about me. I am transitioning from surviving to living.

Notes

All wound up.

Here's the plan; we have to repair, replenish or even replace some concepts and fundamental values we have on the inside. It is so easy to see the need to rehabilitate our bodies but our spirit and our mind is kind of tough. What kale smoothies do we have for that?

The core of man begins in your soul. It is that invisible control center that holds who we really are, our mind, thoughts, emotions, values and attitudes. The mind is complicated. It operates through tools of perception: the senses, knowledge, and memories. These tools are interdependent. How I interpret what I see is based on the information I believe that empowers me to identify it and how I handle it depends on whether I remember this thing to be harmless or harmful. Think about that for a minute before reading the next page. Memories can haunt you or give you something to look forward to.

I'm concerned about the ghosts looming in your house. You know the past situations that you play over and over in your mind. The things that rob your rest and steal your focus. The way you stare off into space in the middle of a conversation as if you traveled back in time and left us with your casing to entertain until you return. Let's work on that. Say this to your self:

My Past is My History, My Present is My Opportunity and My Future is My Destiny

These are the words I wrote to myself everyday when I realized that living in the the past robbed me of the chance to do something special in my present. There is nothing about the events of my past that I have the capacity to physically change. That truth also opened me up to the fact that I was being crippled by fear , afraid of being decisive because I had lost trust in my ability to produce due to poor choices.

While regret and guilt will keep us frozen in our past; fear creates a barricade to our future. Those "what ifs" born out of "what was" keeps you bound and while persons are busy fighting spirits God is screaming at us to loose our souls and let them go. God freed me when He reminded me that the future is His concern. Anything He said about me it is not my job to bring it to pass because it was not my idea in the first place. Furthermore what God said about my future was declared with the understanding of the mishaps, missteps and mistakes along the way. So being obsessed about my future will only result in me ignoring the things I am responsible for right now. I know you are trying to console yourself with what's next but let's balance this out with what's going on right now. At this moment you have already taken a couple breaths to energize you to read this material and as you are cognitively engaged, new ideas are being formed.

You may have lost a lot of stuff along the way but your didn't lose your mind. God preserved your ability to process, create and activate through decisive actions. The same thing that is working against you can work for you if you realize you have not lost your power to decide. Re-frame it! Mistakes give us practical examples of what not to do. Hurt alerts us to the human capacity to be deceptive and brings us into maturity. Abuse reminds us that we are stronger than the things we survive because what was meant to kill us did not. When are you going to agree with the fact that you are still here. Your body has not stopped growing can you allow your soul the opportunity to grow? You see your soul is the indestructible component; your body is just a shell, a casing and although it hurts to lose function in your body; your mind can never lose the real you. Take back your power and evict those robbers out of your mind and be present, show up today.

Can you imagine what will happen if you let out your mind from the cage of guilt? Can you imagine if by faith you get into agreement with God and give yourself a chance to embrace an opportunity? The truth is there are many failures on the way to mobility and thats not a cliche. Have you ever seen your son, daughter, niece or nephew or that kid you've magically become a relative to learning to walk? The child is actively developing the mechanism to achieve mobility but does not have complete understanding of the operation. Wobble, balance, wobble, drop... giggle cry crawl get up repeat. We are not on the sidelines telling this child that they are not meant to be a walker and maybe they should try something else? Where is an emoji when you need one. Can you feel my eyes staring at you right now. So tell me why we do that to ourselves? Why do we shut down our opportunities in the times of our soul's infancy?

A part of what make you alive is growth and just as your body is developing your mind is on a path of growth too.

BUT!!

Are you willing to face the idea that maybe the body is grown but the mind has not grasped the maturity to deal with pain in a healthy way? So my solution is to grow beyond the place of pain and handle it like a champ. Honey I made the decision one day on my little cream leather couch that this pain was going to build me not break me and who I was is no use to the world tied up.

When I thought about Lazarus dead in disappointment eaten up by all the vermin who drew sustenance from his hurt. Mocking his relationship with a God that did not show up at the convenience of their expectations. Lord Jesus.. but God stepped in when man had sealed his stench behind the stone of embarrassment, and spoke to his soul, the real guy and the body had to work with it.

And when he thus had spoken, he cried with a loud voice, Lazarus, come forth. And he that was dead came forth, bound hand and foot with graveclothes: and his face was bound about with a napkin. Jesus saith unto them, Loose him, and let him go.

John 11:43-44 KJV

In the midst of my death God called me and I answered but I was still looking through the grave clothes. Still wrapped up by mistakes. Still smelling the stench of my errors although God had already healed me. Not agreeing with God that every part of my being was functional enough to be everything I was created to be. Still holding myself to the expectations of those who met me at my funeral but were never acquainted with my development and so God began a series of encounters that unwrapped me. Persons who spoke into who I really was that began removing layers until I was free.

They never announced themselves. Never sought fame. Never looked to claim to be the one responsible for my freedom. They just obeyed the Master to take off the things that were stuck to me and helped me let go of the bandages I had gripped.

It may start with prayer but God has assigned someone to speak to those places in your life that are tightly wound. They won't be spooky they might not even say much but even through acts of kindness they remind you that your hands can hold something good and not lose grip. That the same boldness that cause you to move out of your past to say yes to God has been given to others to loose you. It's only a matter of time until those grave clothes come off. All you are required to do is go take a bath and suit up for your opportunity when the time comes. Smell like a solution. Smell like a kingdom kid and put on a garment that gives you the freedom to be exactly who He called you to be.

Let's do the Work!

Believe it!

Prayer Time

Lord I activate my faith now in Your will
for my life. Nothing has happened by
accident and my pain will propel my
purpose as healing is my portion by the
grace of God. I shift out of dormancy into
activity in Jesus name ,,, AMEN

Declaration

I will be everything God Calls me to be on time on schedule and in order. My mishaps, mistakes and miseries were on schedule and God never lost control.

Notes

The best repair is in the
hands of the inventor

Our spirit is the element that makes us alive. It is a whisper of eternity that God breathed into us to connect us to His life giving power. Our spirit knows that our existence here in this life is not permanent and returns to God when our time is up. So every person has a little clock. God created time for us to manage our moments. Even when you're soul is in a frozen state of pain your spirit does not stop ticking. The phrase "Don't waste time " is a cry from our spirit telling us that life is still rolling even when we're still stuck.

 To be in true alignment, our soul must operate in harmony with our spirit and our spirit must be in harmony with God. Something special happens when you give your life to God. He repairs the damage that sin has done to our spirit, puts the soul back into alignment to move forward at the pace of His will. When you understand that God created you intentionally and on purpose. Listen, God wanted those genes to create you exactly the way you look with those skills you currently possess.

Stop complaining about your deficits and get intimate with what God has given you to bring to the table and own it. If you take a deeper look the mission of sin was to deplete you, to cause you to abandon your power, to cause distance in the relationship between you and God because the enemy knows if he can get you hurt enough, bitter enough, lonely enough you will make choices that separate you from your purpose and make you feel that you cannot be fruitful, manage or replenish what you have been made to do but the devil is a liar!

God replaces that breath that was corrupted by sin with Himself. So that His grace can wash our mistakes and empower us to live above life's crushing moments. All Jesus wants is that we release our faith. Faith surpasses our senses, our knowledge and our memories to access God's best for us. Better is possible, wholeness is possible, joy is possible but will you believe?

He that believeth on me, as the scripture hath said, out of his belly shall flow rivers of living water.
John 7:38 KJV

If you have the courage to believe God and receive Him for real in your life not only does He become your source but out of your soul, out of your mind, out of your thoughts is going to flow some life that is going to affect every person you come in contact with. I know some of you may be saying to me but Tiff I already got saved, I've already been baptized but baby it is when you experience God for yourself in the lowest point of your life and see Him pick you up and literally make something out of nothing that you know God is real. This may or may not be the hardest thing you will face in life but God is developing your capacity to endure hardness and still be productive and still have dominion. We have an advantage on the inside: The creator of the universe lives right there.

It is so easy to trust in the things that you can see and touch but what if you are trusting pain more that you are believing God? If we have offered our lives to decaying forces of bitterness, guilt, shame or sin they distance our souls from our true life source and keep us in a cycle of death. Have you ever felt like you were dying on the inside? It is an outcry of your soul alerting you that the harmony, the balance is under attack. Jesus offers us an opportunity to take a hit and not lose a tick. Choose to believe that the pain is not permanent and put it down. That same power that you use to unfriend the one that was unkind to you: unfriend the negative self-talk and the mean things you say about yourself and receive the promises of God for your life.

"...let us also lay aside every weight, and sin which clings so closely, and let us run with endurance the race that is set before us..."
Hebrews 12:1b ESV

I'm so glad that God acknowledges that sin is not our only issue but we have weights, things that burden us down and keep us so tightly wound we can't move forward. What is the driving force behind the way you order your life today? What is pushing you?

So many things can become an idol to us even our pain. We don't know when it happens or how it happens we just fall into the trap where we almost become it. Where our entire existence have been given in tribute to our worst moment. It is a trap that shrouds who we are. You can experience a bitter situation but are you becoming a consistently bitter person? Don't grab these moments like they are eternity; give yourself the permission to see more than the trauma and see what God sees.

No, in all these things we are more than conquerors through him who loved us.
Romans 8:37 ESV

I dare you to read the whole chapter ..

What do you have to conquer with God's love? With everything in you CRUSH IT!!

Healing uses forgiveness through the power of grace to erase the decaying forces of bitterness, guilt, shame and sin and restore our soul, our identity, who we really are to life. When we are wronged or have done something wrong we tend to question our worthiness of good or even life itself. Even before the judge's gavel hit the polished wood, we try ourselves in the courts of our mind for any bad decision we have made and sentence ourselves to isolation even death,

BUT!!!

Grace says you may not be worthy but I think you are worth it! God wants you to know that there is hope after error. That vulnerability is not the gateway to hurt... it is actually the gateway to deliverance. Don't let one person let you leave that piece behind but right if now you open your heart to God and receive His peace and let Jesus strengthen the places that need adjustment and keep going. God is inviting you to a place of change to be empowered to handle difficult places with courage

As you read this page something is happening to you. Mercy is reaching beyond the painful words that called you outside of your name even those that were true; that described you at one phase in time. Mercy is telling you that your arms have the power to move from that position into a brand new minute, a new hour, a new day because it is pushing the recompense of your errors away from you and distancing you from your past. You hear that? Every time you hear that tick of a second you have moved further away from the crisis.You are not what they said, your identity is not finalized by your past. Time is not working against you, it is on your side.

Therefore if any man be in Christ, he is a new creature: old things are passed away; behold, all things are become new.
2 Corinthians 5:17 KJV

God is asking you to believe that there's more. Restoration begins with the blueprint. What does God say about you? What did God say about your soul?

God restores our soul by teaching us how to make better decisions through His Word. He formed us with a purpose and He is willing to help us to fulfill it.

Ye have not chosen me, but I have chosen you, and ordained you, that ye should go and bring forth fruit, and that your fruit should remain: that whatsoever ye shall ask of the Father in my name, he may give it you.
John 15:16 KJV

We have not selected our own pieces. We have absolutely no control over what forms us or puts us together but we must actively become intimate with who we are. We are not random, neither are we mistakes but God looked into the universe and determined that we are necessary. Own that! Embody it! Receive it in your heart that YOU my dear are necessary. There is something in this World that you have been created to do and this pain, this pause has not erased it. My friend it is time to make moves towards your destiny and show up with no more barriers walking into purpose like a testimony.

Let's do the Work!

Identify it!

Prayer Time

Lord I thank you for this moment because You have proven to me that You will do whatever it takes to get me back to where I need to be. You loved me when I couldn't face myself and for that You deserve my devotion. I receive the new air you are filling the lungs of my spirit with. Replace me with You that I can live in freedom

AMEN

Declaration

My pause has produced power to walk in the fullness of my potential. Ready or not... Look out world here I come.

Notes

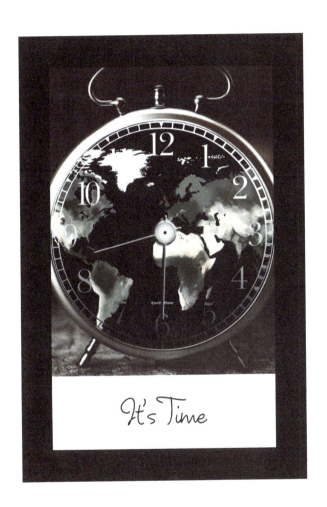

It's Time

For I know the thoughts that I think toward you, saith the Lord, thoughts of peace, and not of evil, to give you an expected end. **Jeremiah 29:11**

Have you ever considered the fact that God knew about your calamity before He called you into purpose. He knew your placement, the time of your pause, the things that would potentially affect you and yet He determined in His heart that the minutes you were created to impact was worth the wait.

Recovery is on your time line. Deliverance is written in your story. Renewal is a part of the plan. Now that you have found all your missing pieces, it is time to give function to the formerly fragmented. The truth is you will log every second every minute differently once you have experienced grace.

For by grace are ye saved through faith; and that not of yourselves: it is the gift of God:
Ephesians 2:8 KJV

The grace to recover was given before the trauma. Grace is the unmerited favor of God distributed out of His unfailing love for us. Consider this, Jesus was already locked in the lineage before the serpent ever played mind games with Eve in Genesis 3. Your second chance, your next, your reset was already in you before this thing ever happened. Grace gives us power to push forward, to rise out of depression, to triumph above the trouble and soar.

Whatever you have abandoned by reason of this event by now you know it's time to pursue your purpose. No more wasting any more breaths. Your time is now…. your moment is here! Whatever you put your hands on to do today, give it everything you've got. LISTEN! The season of seeking validation is OVER!

And whatsoever ye do, do it heartily, as to the Lord, and not unto men;
Colossians 3:23 ESV

You cried for this. You survived suicide, mockery, grief, abandonment, molestation, ridicule, slavery, deception, separation, sickness, poverty, addiction, abuse, guilt, shame, depression, anxiety, trauma, tribulation, suffering, dysfunction, disappointment, failure and confusion for this. It's only right that you agree with God and pursue it with everything you've got. Get your clock in sync with God's time. God is not going to have you cycle back to where you paused but there is an acceleration in the reset. You will move through those seasons at rapid speed to get to where your spirit has been tracking, to where life is moving and then you will receive power to operate in it.

But you will receive power when the Holy Spirit has come upon you, and you will be my witnesses in Jerusalem and in all Judea and Samaria, and to the end of the earth."
Acts 1:8 ESV

God is giving you power in the very place you were betrayed, in the very spot you were buried and He will spread your influence beyond the site of your death even beyond everyplace that was acquainted with your downfall. God is reintroducing you to the world without the baggage, without the barriers and giving you power to walk through the walls of others and bring them life. You might encounter those that might doubt you along the way, trying to figure out if you're being real. If they ask you any questions, I want you to know there is power in your scars.

So the other disciples told him, "We have seen the Lord." But he said to them, "Unless I see in his hands the mark of the nails, and place my finger into the mark of the nails, and place my hand into his side, I will never believe." Eight days later, his disciples were inside again, and Thomas was with them. Although the doors were locked, Jesus came and stood among them and said, "Peace be with you." Then he said to Thomas, "Put your finger here, and see my hands; and put out your hand, and place it in my side. Do not disbelieve, but believe." Thomas answered him, "My Lord and my God!"

John 20:24-28 ESV

Listen, you cannot invite someone into your scars while you are still hanging on the cross. Yes, the crowds will gather but the scars will not put on their full meaning until you get up. It is when you have risen above the trauma, when your wounds have been healed, that you speak from an empowered place. The empowered place gives hope to the wounded that this is not the end. The empowered place gives you courage to face challenges knowing that you have not only survived but lived after tragedy. There were many times I was questioned when was I going to write my story. When was I going to turn my trauma into triumph but the truth is I was not healed yet and my words would only have power if I gave myself and my family an opportunity to heal. God had to teach me that I was able to give birth after that and that our lineage would continue not only in my daughter Jodi but in my son Tyson. So many times during that pregnancy I was afraid that I would lose another child, that God would not trust me with anymore but He showed me I could do it.

I had to know that the love that Odane and I shared could survive anything and the dream that bonded us together to continue the legacy of faith that our parents gave us did not die when Kimberly died but still lives today and will live in these pages when I'm gone and in the hearts of our children. The fact that you are reading this book means I made it to the other side of grief, the other side of pain, the other side of heartache, the other side of terrible mistakes.

The words that you are reading are pieces of evidence that you can live again, love again, dream again. I am the Lazarus walking into your Jerusalem agreeing with Jesus that you will rise again. Having read all this, it's up to you to decide what to do next.

BUT!!!

If I were you... I would get to ticking and

#CRUSHTHEDAY

Let's do the Work!

Crush it!

Prayer Time

Lord thank you for waiting on me and walking with me to this point. I realize I could not make it without You and so Your Love has not just lifted me, it is my motivation to do my very best in everything I do in honor of what You have done for me.

AMEN

Declaration

I was born to win. I have everything it takes and now I give myself the permission to CRUSH THE DAY!!

Notes

To every person God used to

unwrap me....

Thank You

xoxo

#TIFFYGABS 💋